THE BRITISH MUSEUM

Arabic Calligraphy

Naskh script for beginners

Introduction
Venetia Porter

Text and calligraphy
Mustafa Ja'far

THE BRITISH MUSEUM PRESS

A very great word of thanks ...

... to Dr Venetia Porter, The British Museum,
without whose valuable suggestions this booklet would have had many gaps.

... to Jawdat Haseeb Albanna, Madrid, Spain,
for his remarks on and genuine enthusiasm for this booklet.

... to Saleh Salman, Kuwait,
for his generous supply of reed pens, books and other calligraphic materials and resources.

... and to Nawfal Al-Janabi, Abu Dhabi, United Arab Emirates,
for providing me with many valuable books about Arabic calligraphy.

Cover design concept:
Jawdat Haseeb Albanna

Design and illustrations:
Mustafa Ja'far
Arabigraphy.com

First published in 2002 by The British Museum Press
A division of The British Museum Company Ltd
The British Museum
Great Russell Street, London WC1B 3DG

britishmuseum.org/publishing

Reprinted 2005, 2006, 2008, 2009, 2010, 2012, 2013, 2014, 2015, 2018 , 2020

A catalogue record for this book is available from the British Library

ISBN: 978-0-7141-1499-6

Cover illustration by Mustafa Ja'far
Typeset in Humanist
Printed in Dubai by Oriental Press

FSC www.fsc.org
MIX
Paper from responsible sources
FSC® C004800

Introduction

Arabic is both a language and a script. Originally, as a purely spoken language, it was used at the courts of the powerful Arab tribal confederations such as the Lakhmids and the Ghassanids, who were famed for their tradition of oral poetry. These confederations were based in southern Iraq and Syria, lands which were ruled by the Byzantines, who controlled the Mediterranean countries, and by the Sasanians, who ruled Iraq and Iran. With the birth of the Islamic state in Arabia after AD 622, these lands eventually became part of the Islamic empire. Arabic belongs to the same family of scripts as Hebrew, Greek and Latin, all of which derive ultimately from the Phoenician alphabet developed in the late second millennium BC. The origin of the Arabic letter shapes is still a matter of scholarly debate, but it seems most likely that they are derived from the form of Aramaic script used by the Nabataeans, whose sumptuous capital, Petra, still survives in present-day Jordan.

Arabic was the language in which the Qur'ān, the Holy Book of the Muslims, was revealed through the intermediary of the Archangel Gabriel to the Prophet Muḥammad outside Mecca in the early seventh century AD, and the script in which it was subsequently written down. The language and the script were thus endowed with great sanctity, and every effort was made when copying the Qur'ān and other religious texts to write as beautifully as possible. In the early period, the style of script used for religious texts and subsequently for monumental inscriptions was an angular one, commonly known as Kufic. Everyday correspondence, at that time on papyrus, was written in a more rounded cursive script. The angular script, which, by the twelfth century, had become increasingly elaborate and embellished, was gradually superseded by more legible cursive scripts, one of which was Naskh.

The expansion of Islam from Spain to the west, into Africa and as far east as Indonesia led to the widespread diffusion of the Arabic language and script. Because it is incumbent upon Muslims to read and recite the Qur'ān in its original Arabic, the language was frequently learnt alongside local languages. In many cases the Arabic script displaced local scripts, taking it beyond the sphere of the Arabic language itself. It was employed to write a whole variety of languages such as Persian, Urdu, Dari, Ottoman Turkish (until the reforms of Ataturk in 1928, when the Roman-Turkish alphabet replaced it) and until relatively recently some of the languages of Indonesia and Malaysia. After scripts using the Roman alphabet, Arabic is the most commonly written script in the world.

The Arabic script continues to fascinate and inspire. The famous Persian calligrapher, Mīr ᶜAlī of Herāt (d.1556), gave the following advice to those embarking on the task: 'The calligrapher needs five things: a fine temperament, an understanding of calligraphy, a good hand, the ability to endure pain and a perfect set of implements.'

Venetia Porter
The British Museum

‘Do not be afraid of failure, or indeed of copying too slavishly. Once these processes have become part of your experience, your ***self*** will ensure that the letters become your own.’

Donald Jackson

Naskh script

Naskh, which literally means to copy or the copyist's hand, is one of the six major cursive Arabic scripts, the *al-aqlām al-sittah* (six pens or styles) that were established during the tenth century AD. The origins of Naskh can be traced back to the late eighth century AD, but at that time the script lacked refinement and was used mainly for correspondence.

When Ibn Muqlah, the great Abbasid calligrapher and vizier (d.940), subjected the six cursive scripts to rigorous proportional analysis, Naskh became the most popular script for book copying. However, the elegant refinements which elevated Naskh to the realms of a script suitable for the Qur'ān are usually attributed to Ibn al-Bawwāb (d.1022), the second great calligrapher of the Abbasid period.

In the thirteenth century the style of Ibn al-Bawwāb was made more graceful by Yāqūt al-Mustaᶜṣimī, the last great calligrapher of the Abbasids (d.1298). Yāqūt al-Mustaᶜṣimī was also responsible for making changes to the shape of the reed pen that had a remarkable effect on all six scripts. He steepened the angle of the writing edge of the pen and left it thicker.

In the fifteenth century the Ottoman Turks favoured Naskh as the most congenial script for copying the Qur'ān. They set it apart for this task, labelled it *khādim al-Qur'ān* (servant of the Qur'ān) and raised it to new levels of perfection. But it was not until the nineteenth century that Naskh was to reach its peak, at the hands of Kādīasker Mustafa İzzet Efendi (d.1876) and Mehmed Şevki Efendi (d.1887), in Istanbul. Their supremely beautiful Naskh has inspired calligraphers ever since.

Naskh is still the most widely used Arabic script today, with more Qur'āns copied in it than in all other scripts put together.

The Arabic alphabet

Arabic, like Hebrew and Aramaic, is written from right to left and its alphabet consists of 28 consonants. Short vowels are represented by signs above and below the letters (see page 18). The alphabet is written here in the unjoined forms of the Naskh script. The Roman letters indicate a sound equivalent to that of the Arabic.

The fine grey horizontal rules serve as a base line.

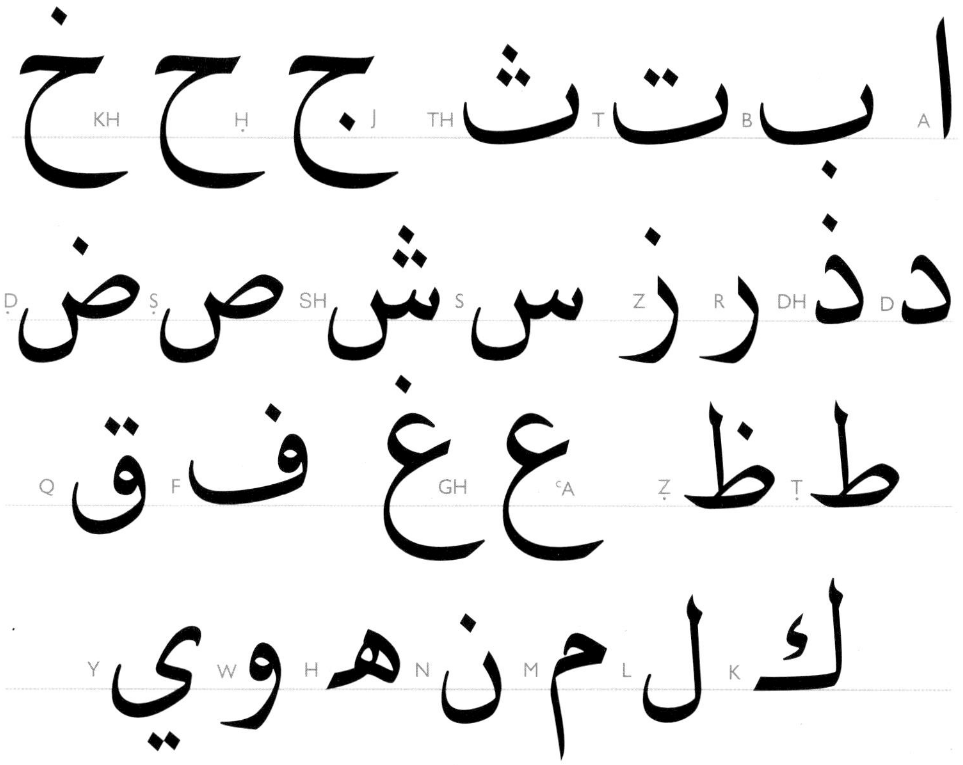

Letter variations

Most Arabic letters vary according to their position in the word (initial, medial or final) and whether they are joined or unjoined. The letters below are the five variations of *hā'* (H) in Naskh script. Some scripts have fewer variations. Some of the variations of each letter are given on the explanatory pages, and some on pages 19 to 21.

Getting started

Today, when it comes to calligraphy tools, we are spoilt for choice. Art shops offer a variety of writing implements, with nibs of steel, glass, nylon fibres, etc, in many different shapes and sizes.
But the best tool for Arabic calligraphy was, and still is, the reed pen. It is not only more practical than most of the ready-made pens, but it is cheaper too. It allows you to create a writing implement that suits your own hand posture and writing angle, rather than having to adapt your hand to a ready-made pen. The ideal reed, which grows in swamps and shallow waters, is prepared only when it is completely dry. It is cut with a heavy-duty knife or scalpel.
Follow these five steps to prepare your first reed pen.

Select a reed stem and cut it to the length of a pen (about 20 cm). The diameter should be around 1cm. If you do not have access to suitable reeds, you can use small bamboo sticks available at garden centres or buy a ready-cut reed pen from an art shop that specializes in calligraphy materials and recut it to the appropriate angle.

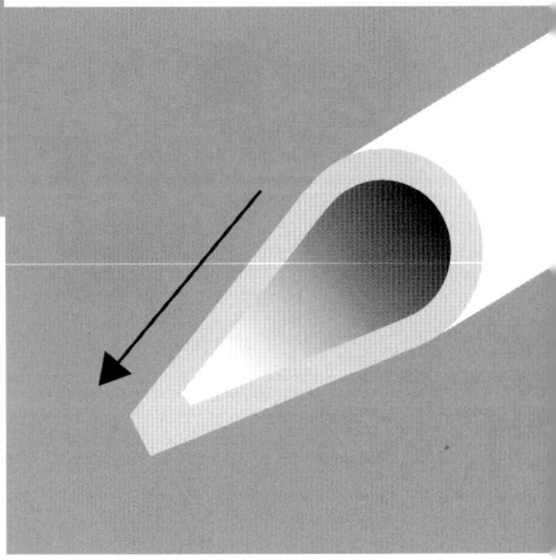

Work at the end furthest from any bulge. Hold the reed firmly and cut away a long scoop using a sharp knife or scalpel.

Writing angle

Before you tackle the alphabet, test your pen by drawing some diamond-shaped dots. The pen should rest comfortably between the lower knuckles of the thumb and the first finger, as in the illustration. Press the pen diagonally on the paper and pull it in the direction of the arrows. When you manage to draw a diamond-shaped dot with a single short diagonal stroke that means you are holding your pen correctly. If not, try again. Make sure the full width of the slanted nib is touching the paper and that your pen is moving in the direction of the arrows. This is the basic writing angle, but when you begin to copy individual letters or words you will find that a certain amount of pen manipulation is necessary to achieve a pleasing contrast of stroke widths.

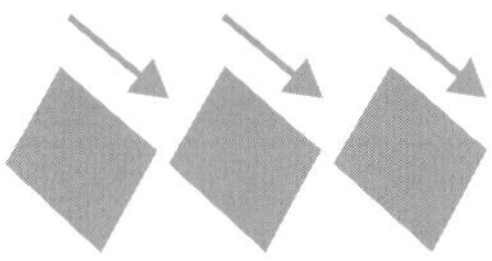

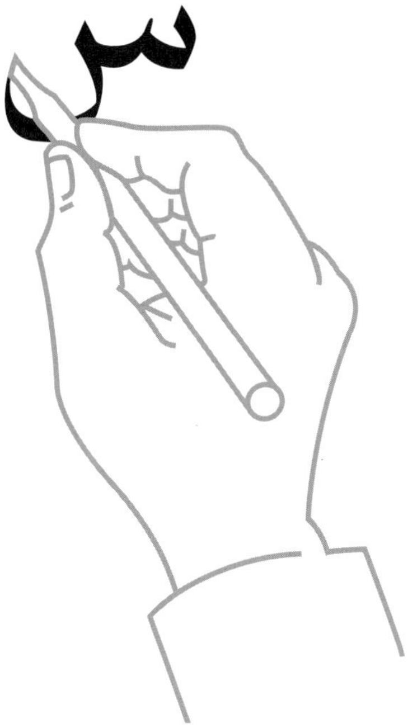

Ink and ink jar

Inks suitable for practising include black Indian ink, Rotring black drawing ink, and any calligraphy ink. In order not to flood the pen you need to make an ink jar. Find a small watertight jar or plastic film container. In the past calligraphers placed a small wad of raw-silk fibres inside the jar, but nowadays a small piece of nylon tights or stockings does just as well. Push this into the jar and pour in enough ink to be completely absorbed by the fabric. No excess ink is required, as the source of ink must be the ink-dampened fabric. This prevents overloading the pen and creating unsightly blobs.

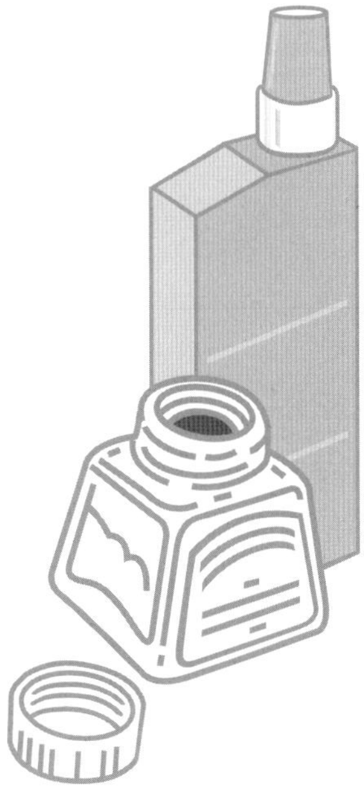

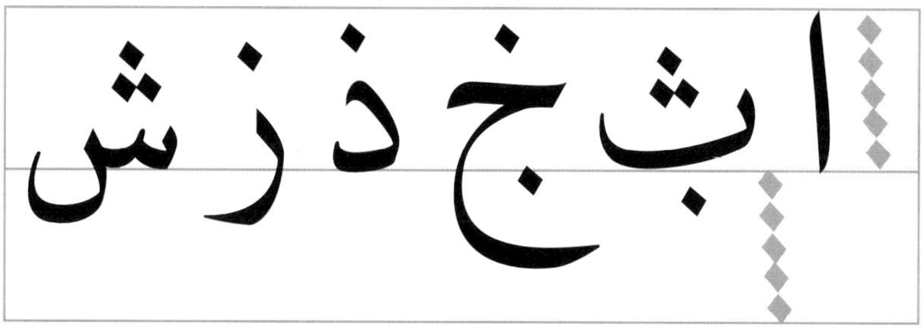

Guidelines

To prepare your practice sheet, use a soft pencil to draw the base line (middle line). Then draw the upper and lower lines at equal distances from the base line using the height of the letter *alif* as a guide. In Naskh script the height of *alif* should equal five dots of your pen placed one on top of the other. Use a white fairly smooth matt paper for practising.

Learning stages

As a beginner, your learning process should be divided into three basic stages, as in this booklet:

1. *Mufradāt* single letters (pages 8-18)
2. *Murakkabāt* joined letters (pages 19-21)
3. *Kalimāt* words (pages 22-25)

You should only move to the next stage when you feel comfortable with the previous one.

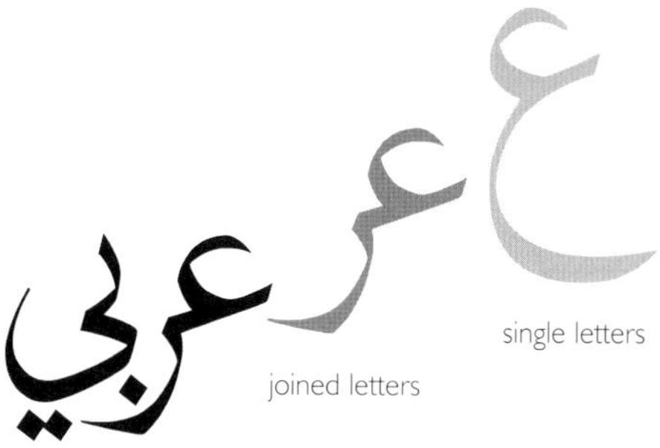

Stroke-by-stroke guide

The unique stroke-by-stroke instructions on the following pages show you the best way of writing each letter of the alphabet. Try to write slowly, following the instructions, and moving your pen in the direction of the arrows.

Extra effort!

Do not despair if you find these four letters extremely difficult to write. They are indeed considered the most arduous of all the letters, and beginners should give them extra effort.

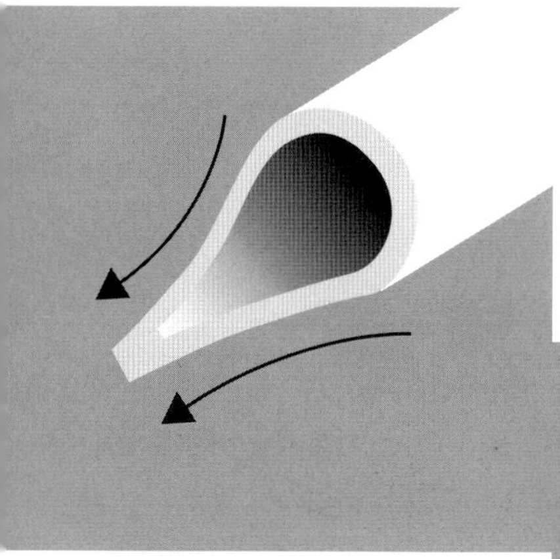

To create the shoulders, make a cut on each side, taking care to create an end with parallel sides. Aim for a nib width of about 4 mm or less.

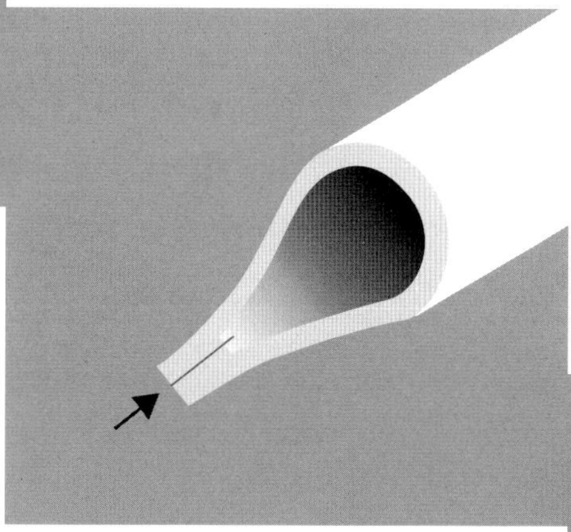

Place the reed on a hard surface. Make a slit down the middle of the the nib. No slit is required if the width of the nib is less than 4 mm.

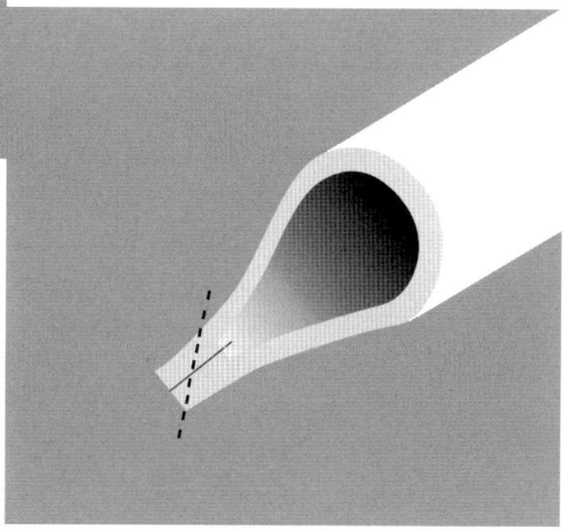

Cut the nib to an angle of about 45°. The angle will depend on your hand and you may have to recut the nib to achieve a satisfactory writing angle. Dip the pen in the ink jar and allow it to absorb plenty of ink before you start.

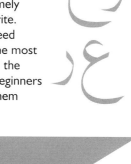

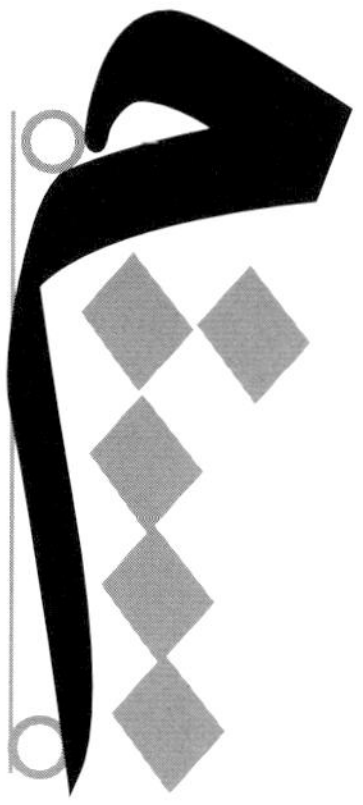

Proportions

Proportioned letters like this are designed to help you appreciate the correct shape of each letter. The diagonal-shaped dot represents one full pen width, while the circle indicates half that width. The proportions should serve as a guide only and need not be strictly adhered to.

Stage One: *Mufradāt* single letters

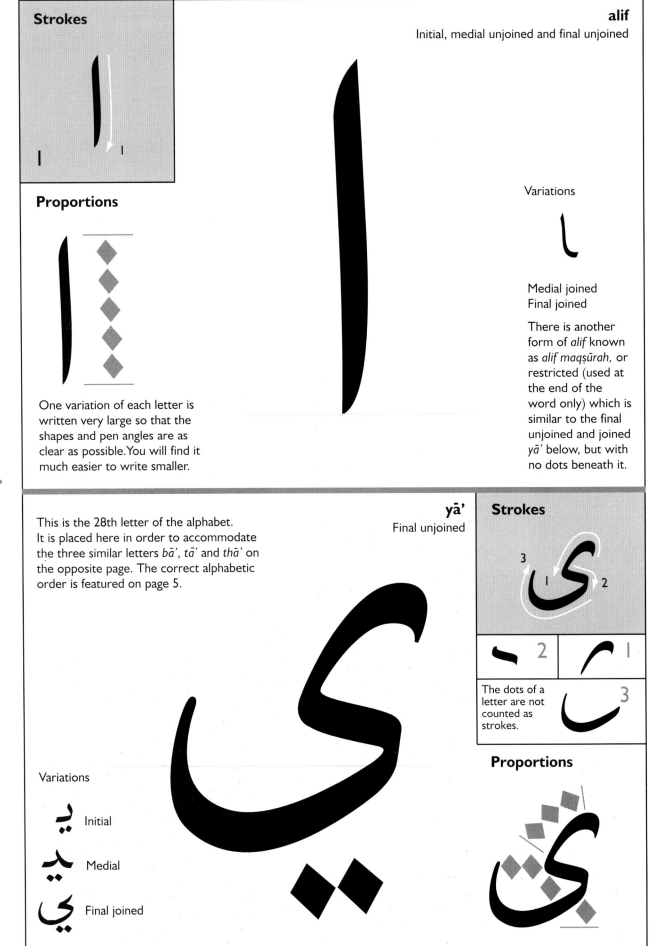

Strokes

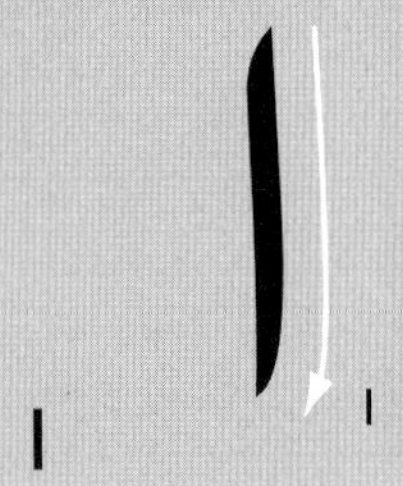

Proportions

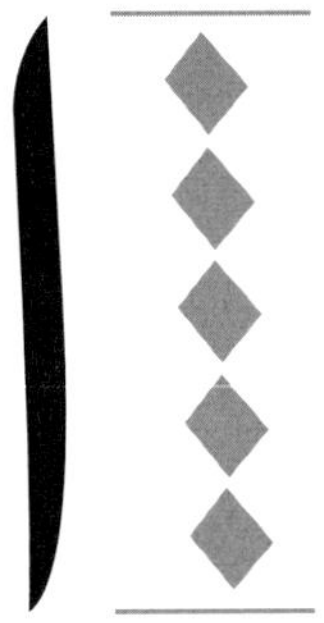

One variation of each letter is written very large so that the shapes and pen angles are as clear as possible. You will find it much easier to write smaller.

alif

Initial, medial unjoined and final unjoined

Variations

Medial joined
Final joined

There is another form of *alif* known as *alif maqṣūrah,* or restricted (used at the end of the word only) which is similar to the final unjoined and joined *yā'* below, but with no dots beneath it.

yā'

Final unjoined

This is the 28th letter of the alphabet. It is placed here in order to accommodate the three similar letters *bā'*, *tā'* and *thā'* on the opposite page. The correct alphabetic order is featured on page 5.

Variations

Initial

Medial

Final joined

Strokes

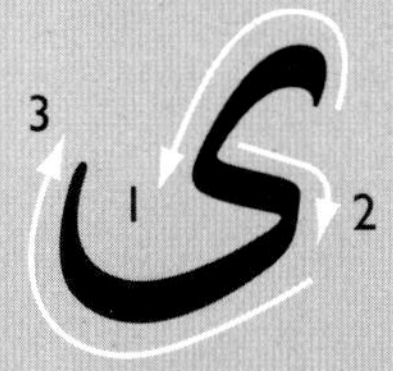

The dots of a letter are not counted as strokes.

Proportions

bā’
Final unjoined

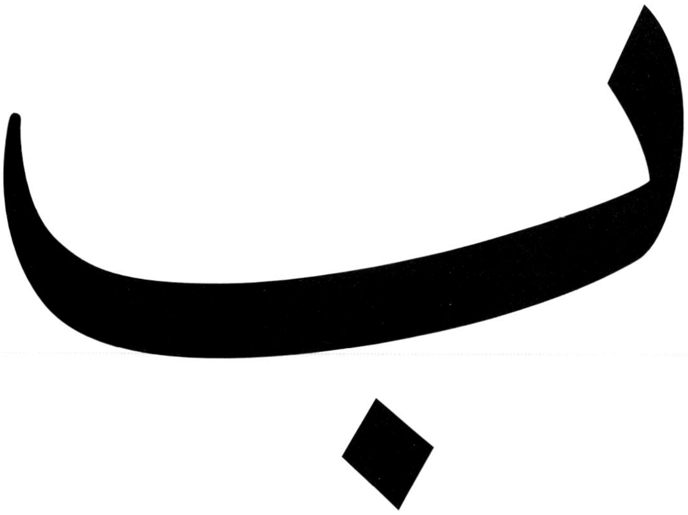

Variations

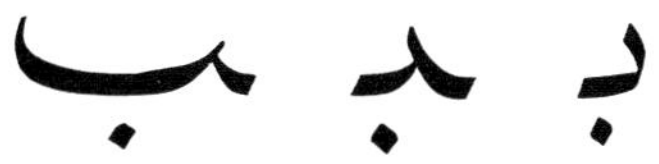

Final joined   Medial   Initial

Strokes

1

2

tā’
Final unjoined

Variation of the letter:
same as **bā’**, but with two dots above and no dot below

Proportions

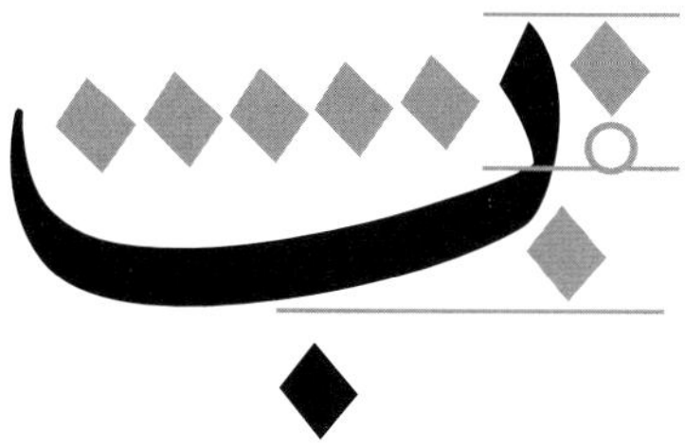

thā’
Final unjoined

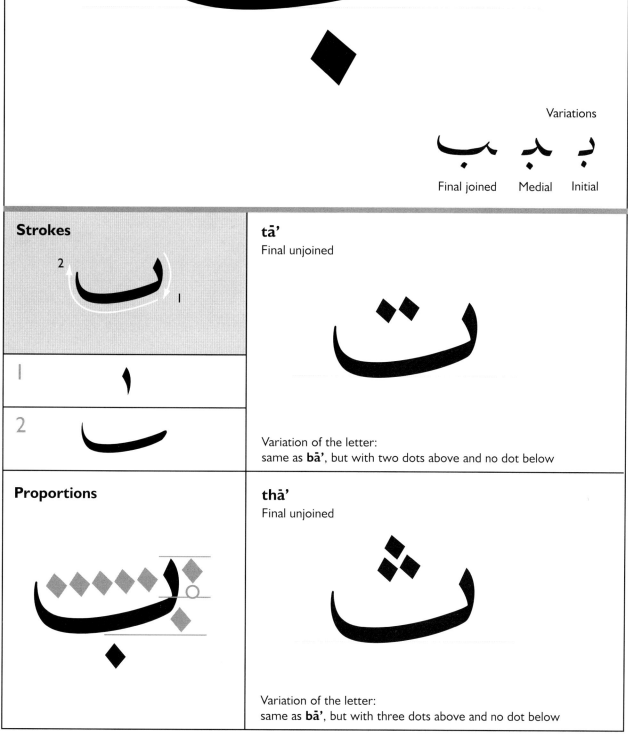

Variation of the letter:
same as **bā’**, but with three dots above and no dot below

jīm

Final unjoined

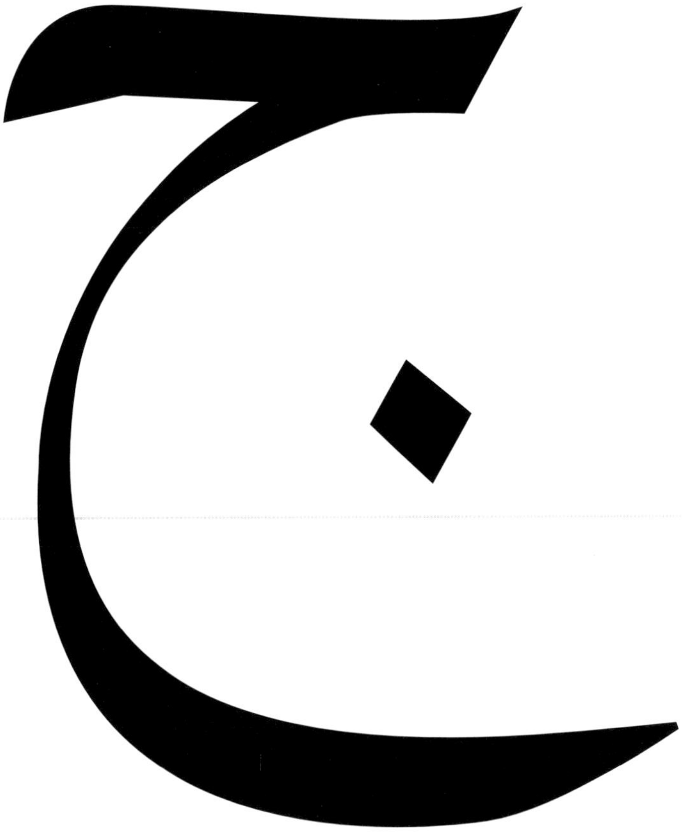

Strokes

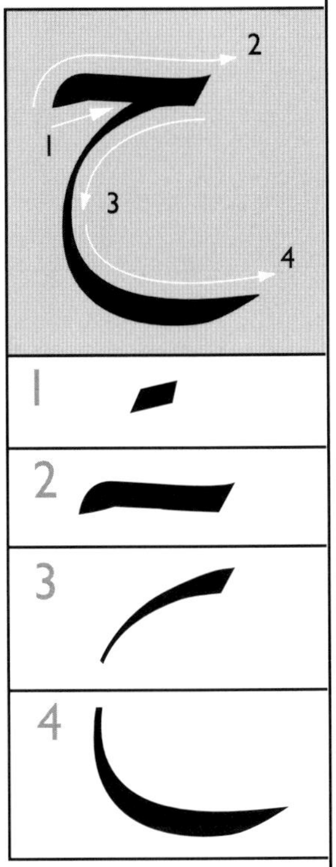

Variations

Final joined Medial Initial

Tip: Use the right corner of your nib to outline and fill in the lower end of the letter marked here in black.

Proportions

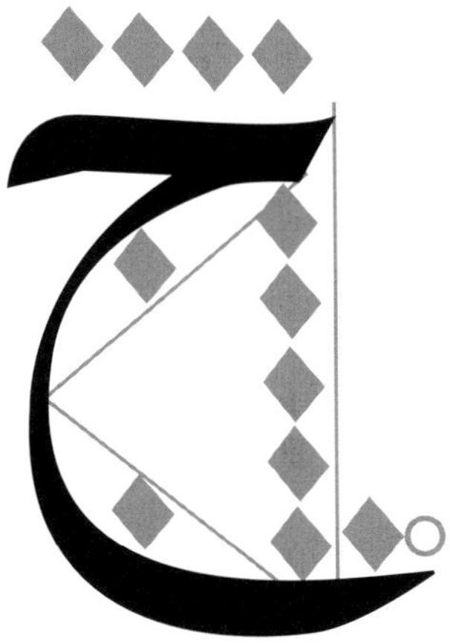

khā' Final unjoined

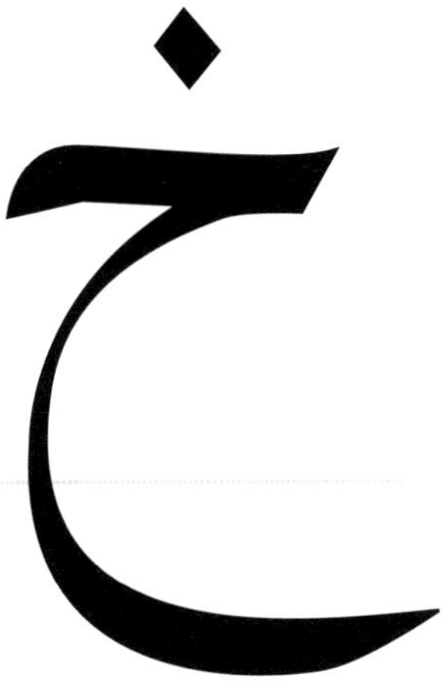

Variation of the letter:
same as **jīm**, but the dot placed above

ḥā' Final unjoined

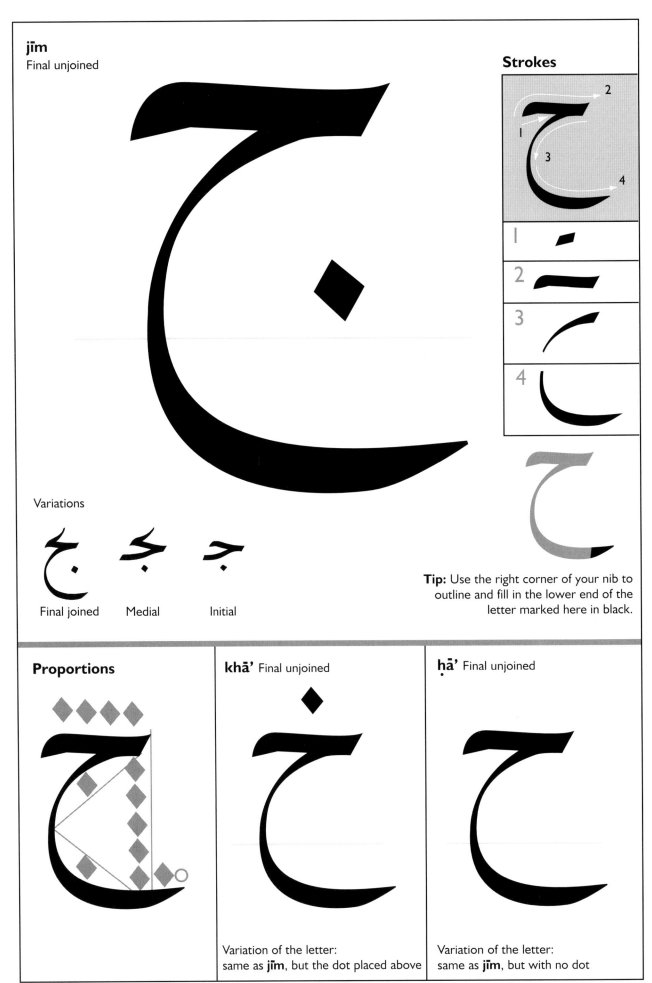

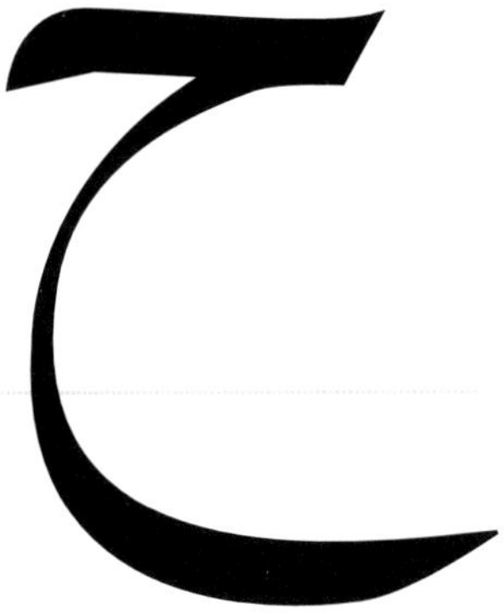

Variation of the letter:
same as **jīm**, but with no dot

Strokes

1 

2 

dāl

Initial, medial unjoined and final unjoined

Variation

Medial joined
Final joined

Proportions

dhāl

Initial, medial unjoined and final unjoined

Variation of the letter: same as **dāl**, but with a dot above

Strokes

1 

2 

zay

Initial, medial unjoined and final unjoined

Variation of the letter: same as **rā'**, but with a dot above

rā'

Initial, medial unjoined and final unjoined

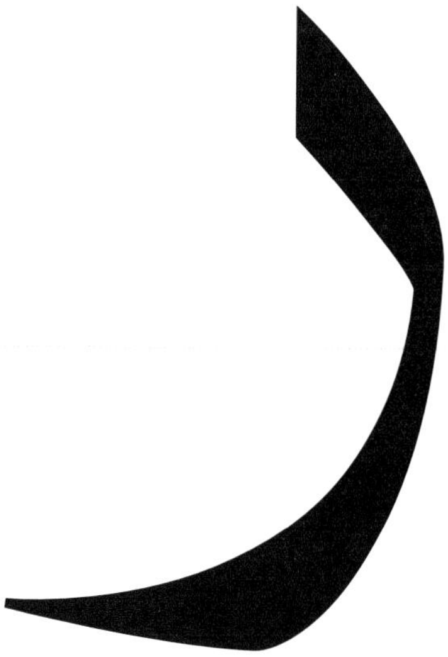

Proportions

Tip: Use the right corner of your nib to outline and fill in the lower end of the letter marked here in black.

Variation

Medial joined
Final joined

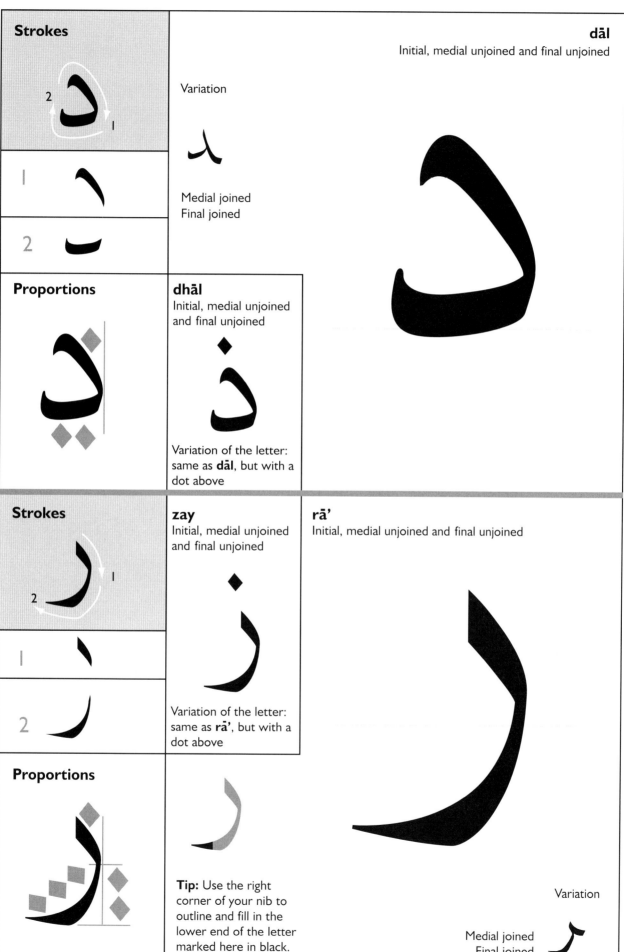

Strokes

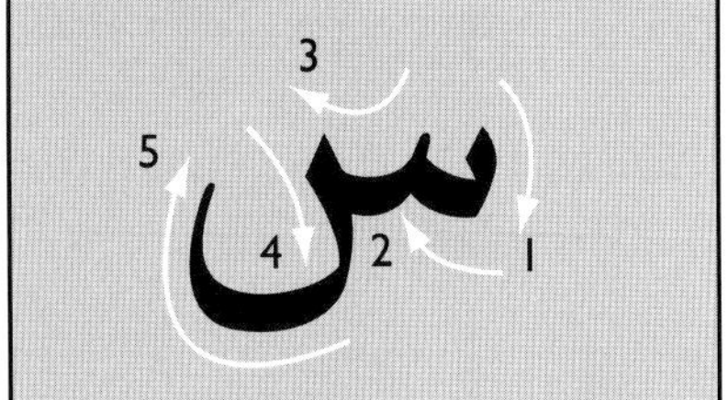

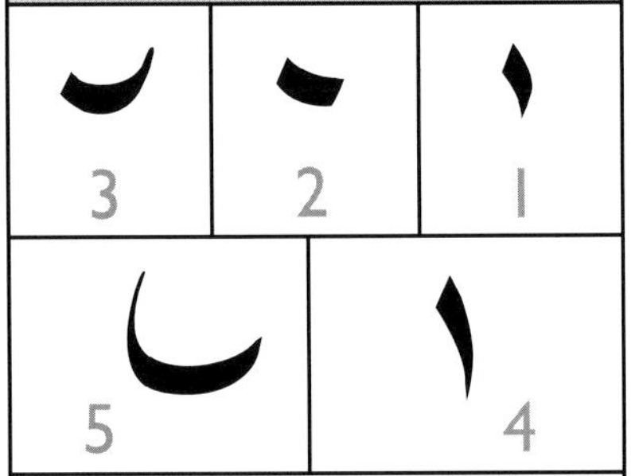

Proportions

sīn
Final unjoined

Variations

Final joined Medial Initial

shīn
Final unjoined

Variation of the letter: same as **sīn**, but with three dots above

Strokes

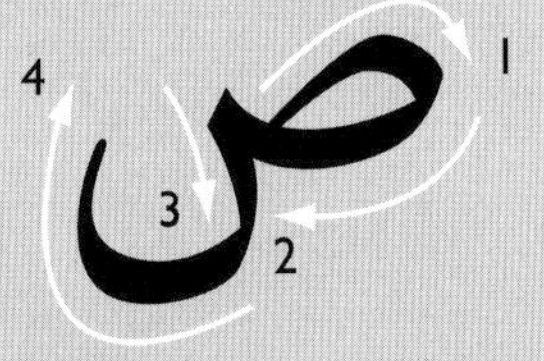

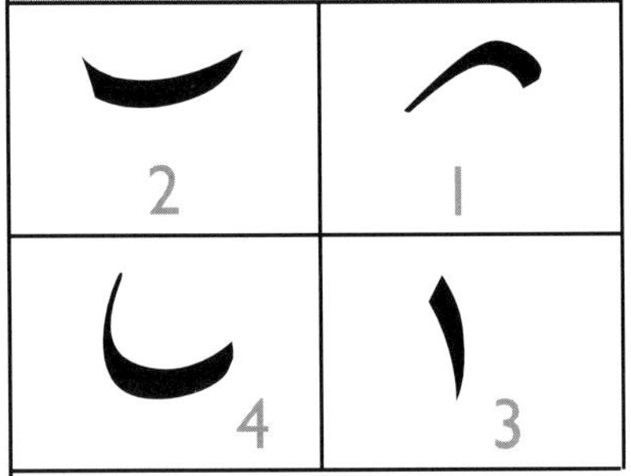

Proportions

ṣād
Final unjoined

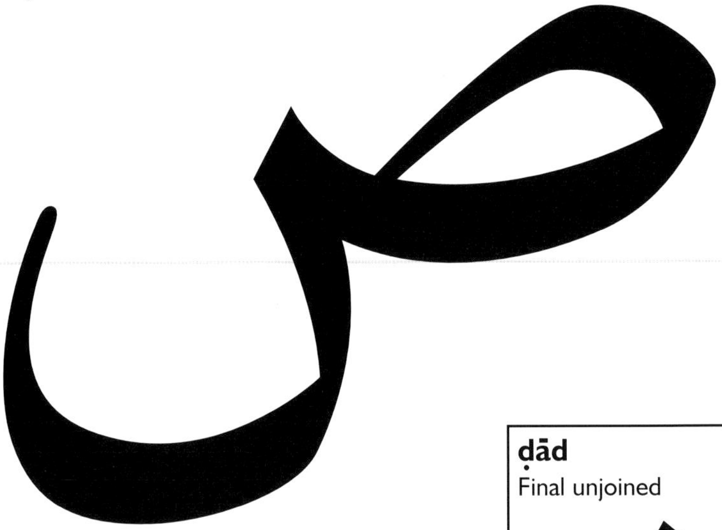

Variations

Final joined Medial Initial

ḍād
Final unjoined

Variation of the letter: same as **ṣād**, but with a dot above

Strokes

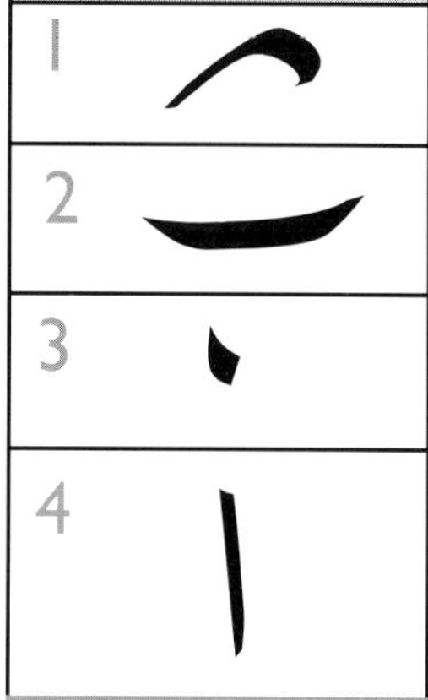

Proportions

ẓā' Final unjoined

Variation: same as **ṭā'** but with a dot above

ṭā' Final unjoined

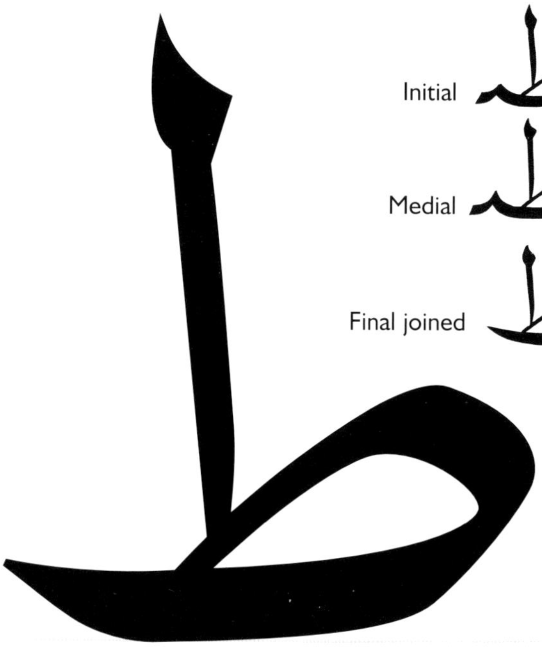

Variations

Initial

Medial

Final joined

Tip: Use the right corner of your nib to outline and fill in the lower end of the letter marked here in black.

'ayn Final unjoined

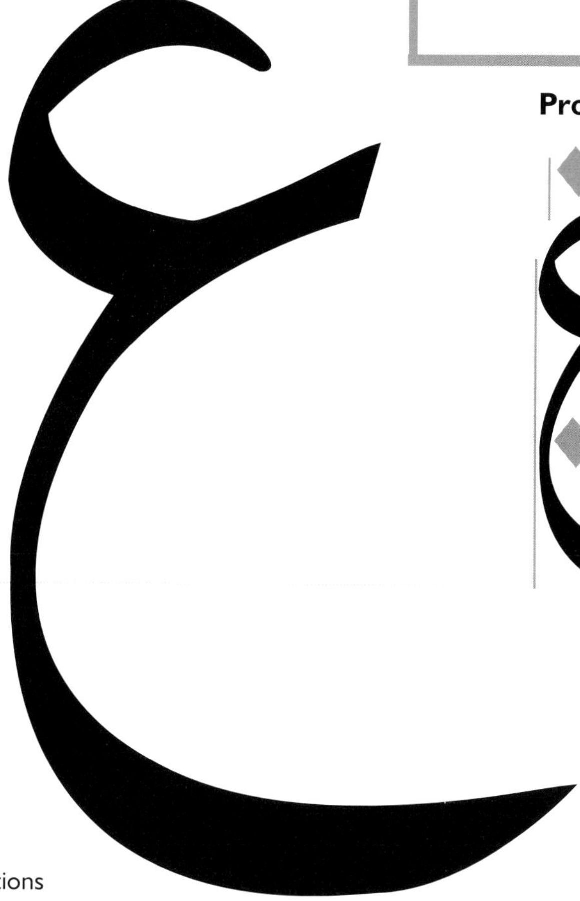

Proportions

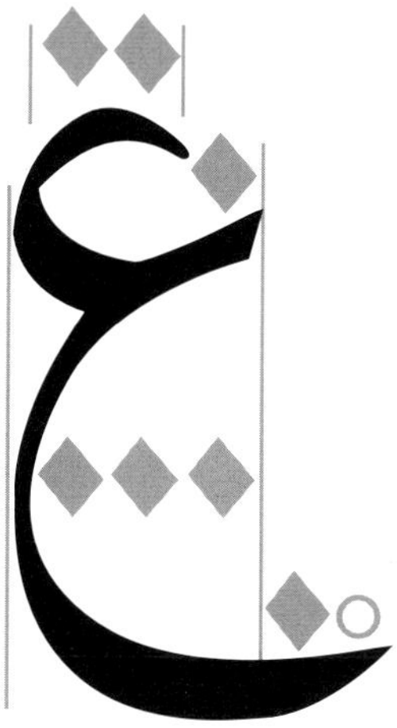

Strokes

Use the right corner of your nib to outline and fill in the crescent.

Tip: Use the right corner of your nib to outline and fill in both the top crescent and the lower end of the letter marked here in black.

ghayn
Final unjoined

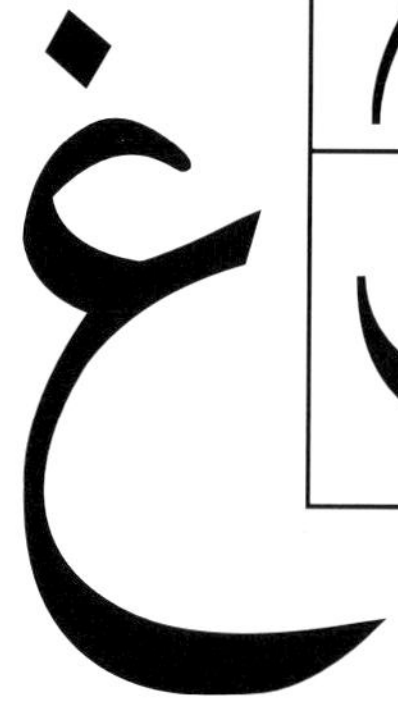

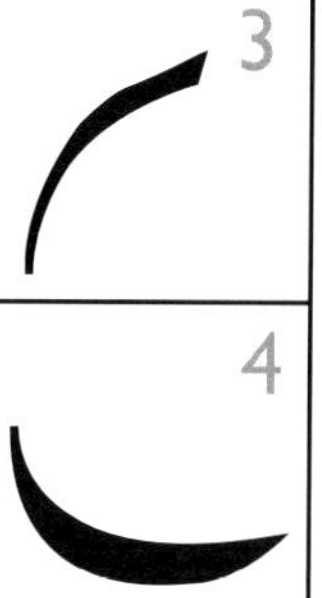

Variation: same as **'ayn**, but with a dot above

Variations

Final joined

Medial

Initial

Strokes

Proportions

fā’ Final unjoined

Variations

Final joined Medial Initial

Strokes

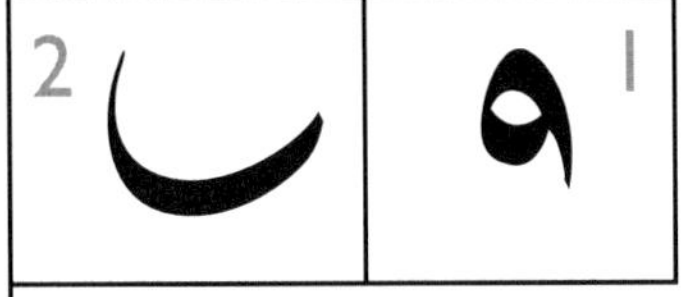

Proportions

qāf Final unjoined

Variations

Final joined Medial Initial

kāf

Final unjoined

Strokes

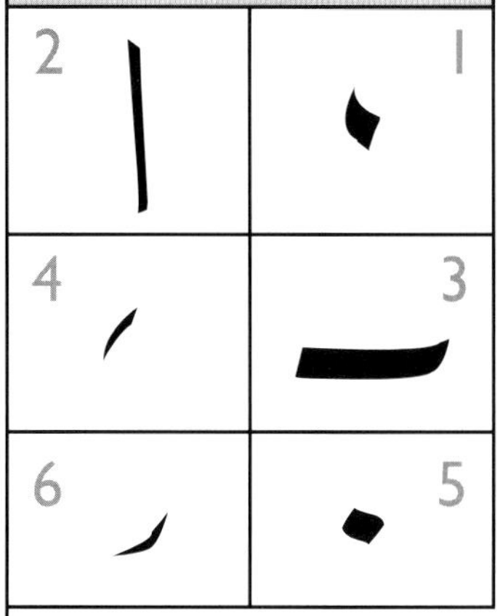

Tip: Use the right corner of your nib to outline and fill in the end of this special *hamzah* of the letter **kāf**.

Proportions

Variations

Initial

Medial

Final joined

For further variations of initial and medial forms of the letter **kāf** see pages 19 and 20.

lām Final unjoined

Proportions

Variations

Initial

Medial

Final joined

Strokes

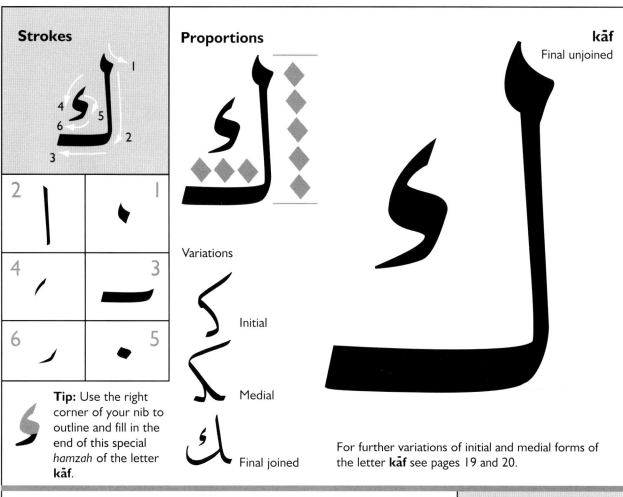

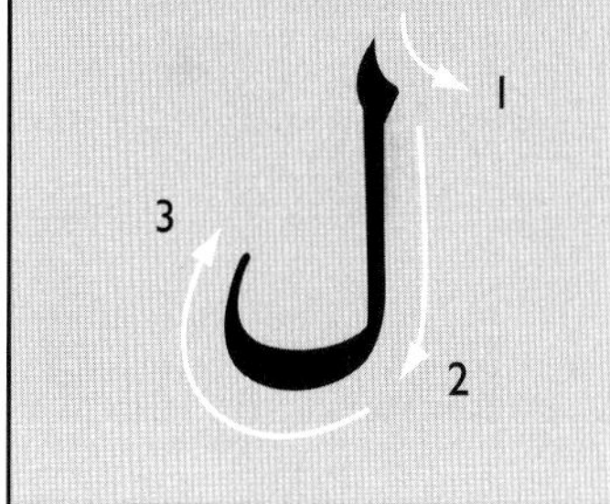

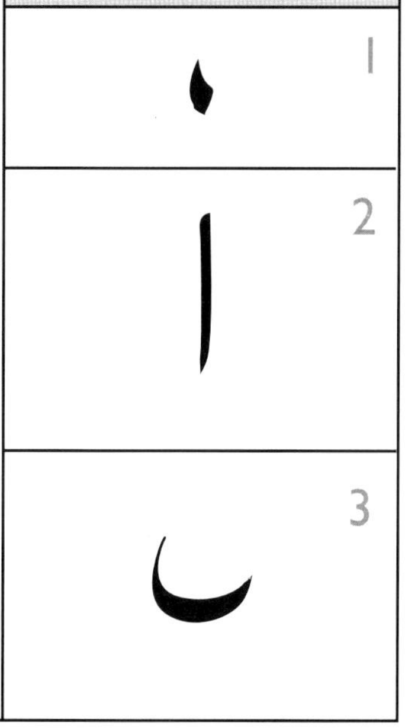

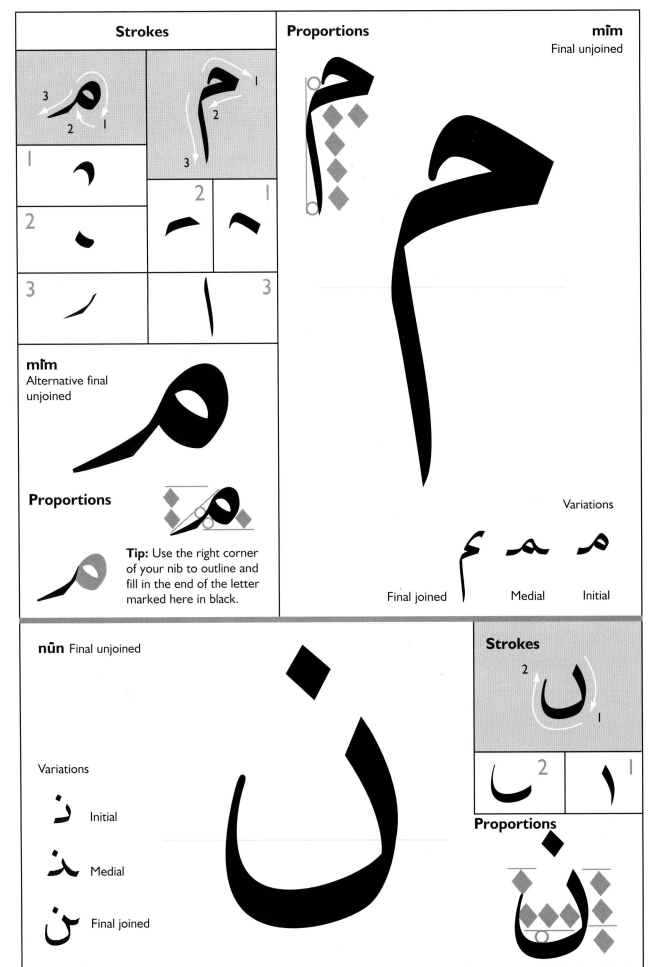

Strokes

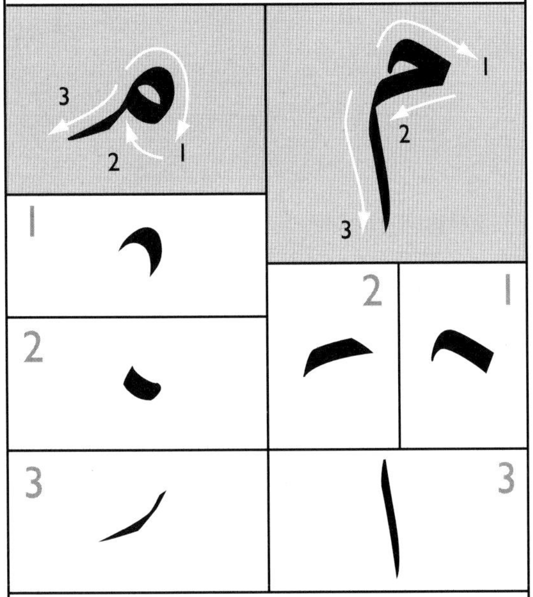

Proportions

mīm
Final unjoined

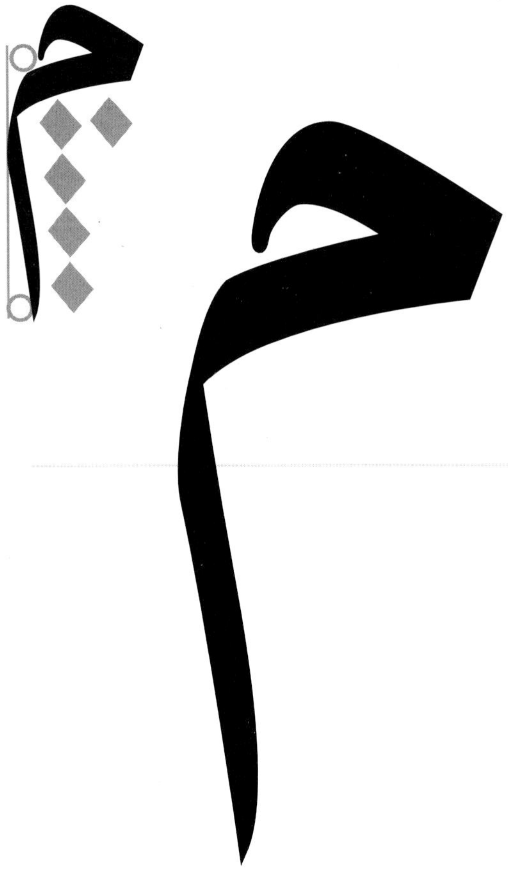

mīm
Alternative final unjoined

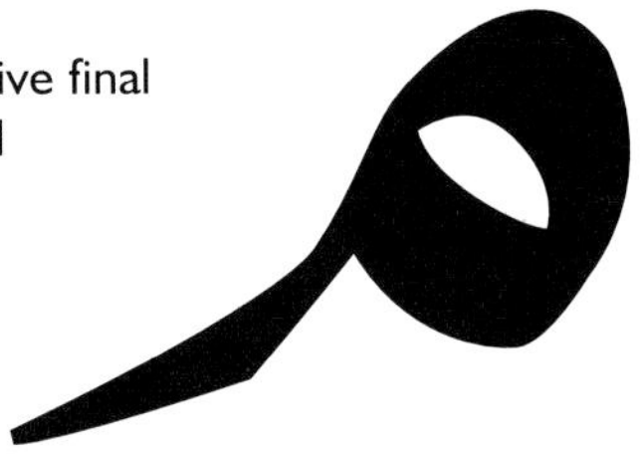

Proportions

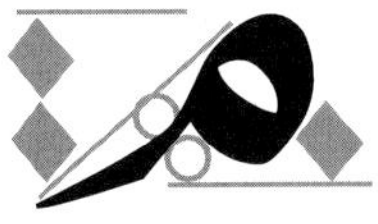

Tip: Use the right corner of your nib to outline and fill in the end of the letter marked here in black.

Variations

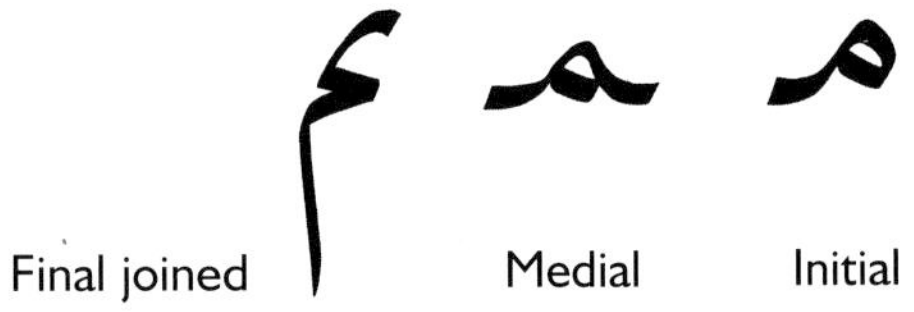

nūn Final unjoined

Strokes

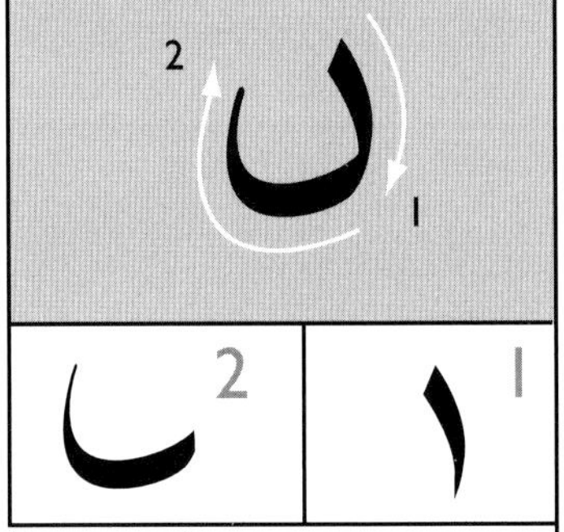

Proportions

Variations

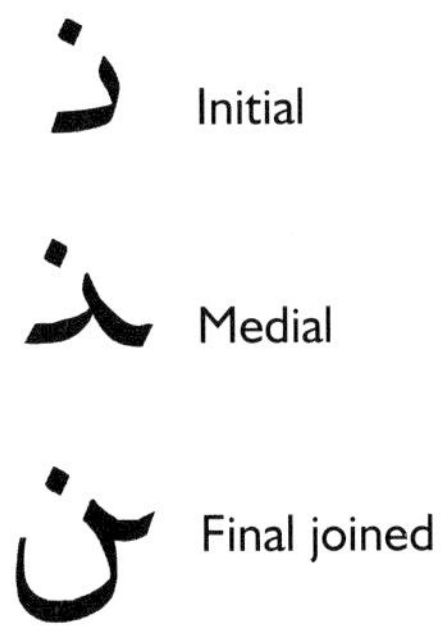

hā'
Initial

Strokes

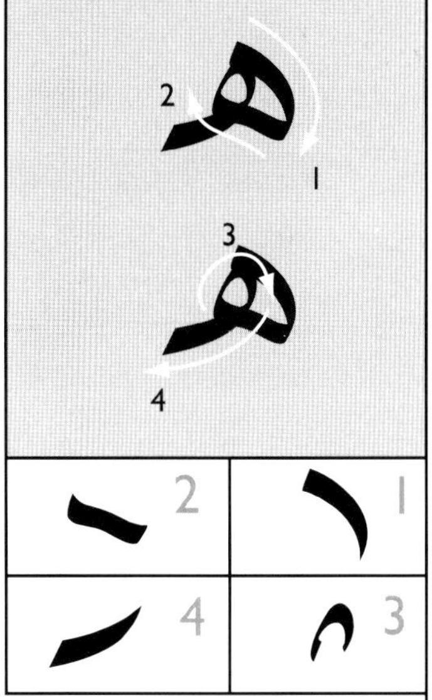

Variations

 Medial

 Medial

 Final joined

 Final unjoined

For the proportions of the various forms of this letter see pages 20 and 21.

Proportions

wāw Initial, medial unjoined and final unjoined

Variation

Medial joined
Final joined

Strokes

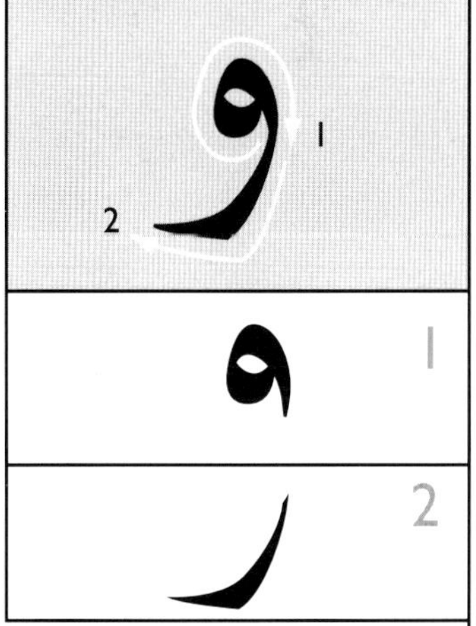

Proportions

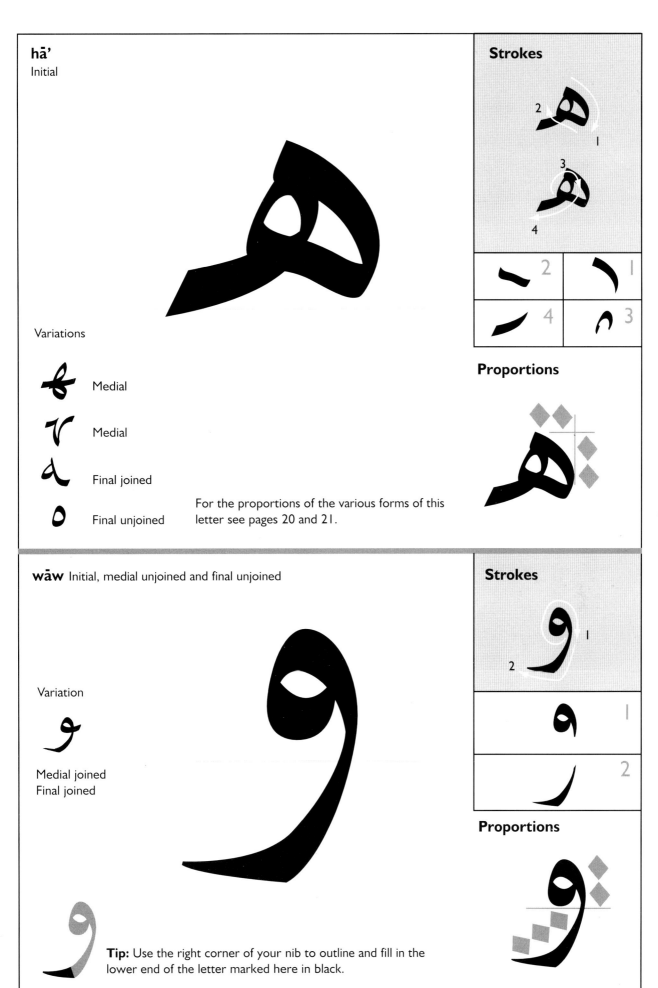

Tip: Use the right corner of your nib to outline and fill in the lower end of the letter marked here in black.

Strokes

Hamzah

Hamzah represents a glottal stop, the sudden closing of the throat as in the London cockney bu'er (butter). It maintains the same shape wherever it appears.

Proportions

Hamzah can be found on its own (1) or combined with other letters (2). When combined, it should be written with a smaller pen.

1 هواء 2 تأثير مؤجل طائرات كفء

Numbers

Numbers Modern Arabs use two systems of number representation (**A** and **B** below). System **A** is used in the eastern part of the Arab world only, while system **B** is currently used in both eastern and western parts.

A	٩	٨	٧	٦	٥	٤	٣	٢	١	٠
B	9	8	7	6	5	4	3	2	1	0

Orthographical signs

Usually written with a smaller pen, the orthographical signs represent short vowels and are positioned above and below the letters according to the grammatical system to indicate that the consonant is followed by *a*, *i*, *u*, etc. They are designed to ensure the exact pronunciation of the text, especially the Qur'ānic verses.
The letter ***bā'*** is used here to demonstrate how the orthographical signs affect pronunciation.

tanwīn maj'rūr	*tanwīn marfūᶜ*	*shaddah*	*sukūn*	*ḍammah*	*kasrah*	*fatḥah*
sound: *bin*	sound: *bun*	sound: doubled BB	sound: vowelless	sound: *bu*	sound: *bi*	sound: *ba*

Decorative signs to be placed above undotted letters such as *sīn* and *rā'*.

Usually placed either above or below the final joined *hā'* to indicate that it is not *tā' marbūṭah* which is similar, but with two dots above. Compare final joined *hā'* (page 17) and *tā' marbūṭah* in the word banner (page 23).

Another sign that may be placed above vowelless consonants.

Sign to indicate that an *alif* must be pronounced even if it is not written.

Decorative signs to be placed beneath the undotted letters *ḥā'*, *sīn*, *ṣād* and *'ayn* respectively. They help the calligrapher to create a visually balanced text.

Maddah, usually placed above *alif* to extend its sound.

Tanwīn manṣub, a grammatical sign that appears above the top end of the final joined *alif* as well as above some other letters.

Hamzat al-alif

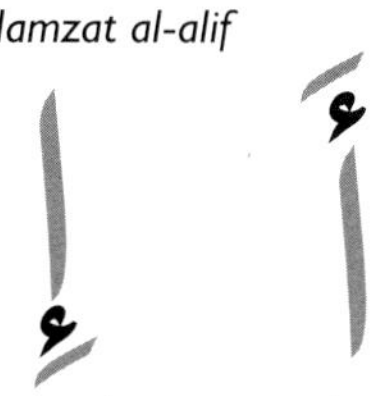

sound: e sound: a'

The use of orthographical signs requires a proper knowledge of Arabic grammar.
Only the most widely used signs are featured here.

Stage Two: *Murakkabāt* joined letters

This section is designed to show as many joined letters as a beginner should need to practise at this stage. To illustrate all forms of joined letters is beyond the scope of this manual.

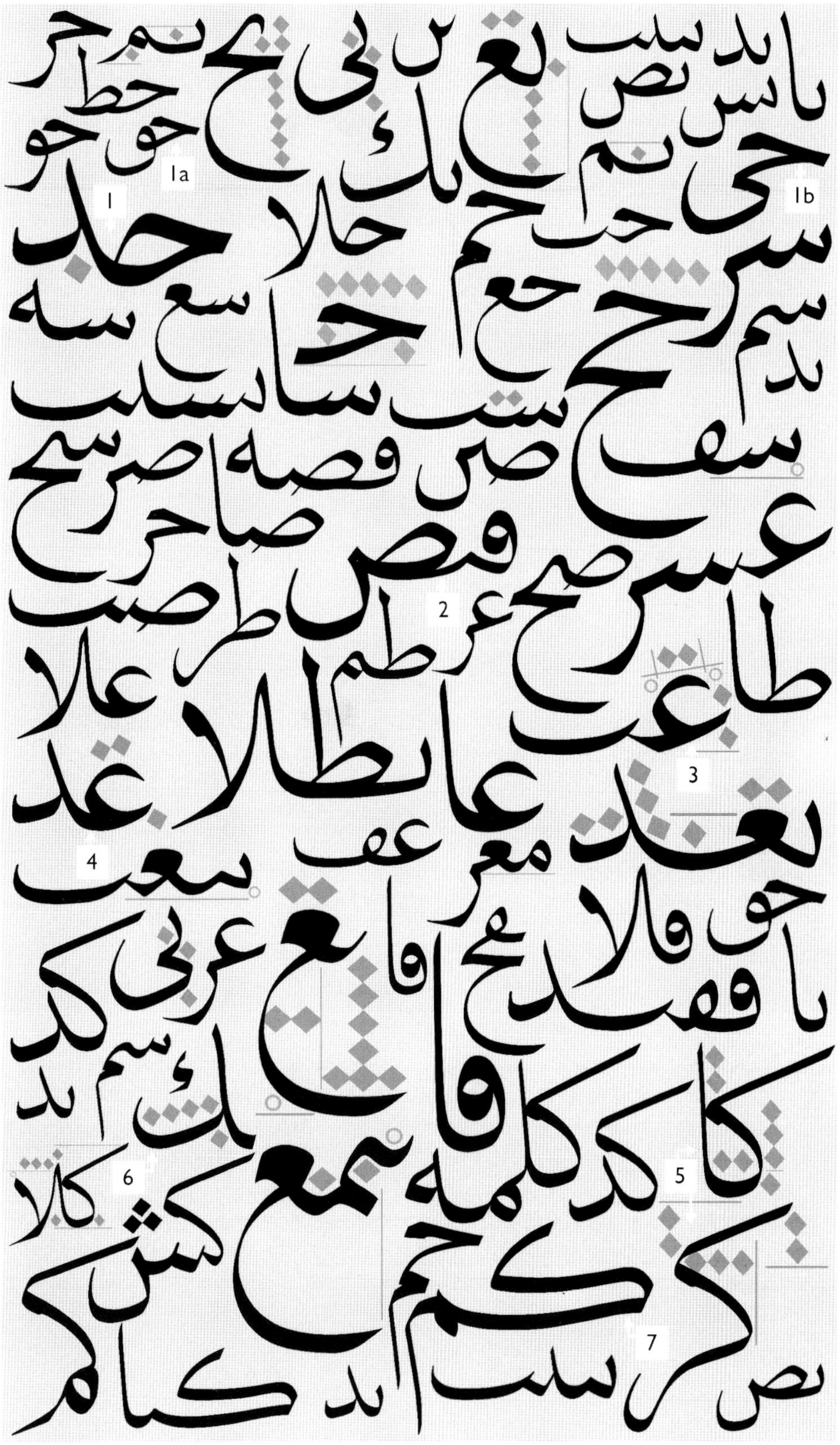

1 Initial *ḥā'* has two different forms:

(a) closed if it is followed by an ascending letter (1).

(b) open if it is followed by a descending letter (1a, 1b).

1 Notice how *dāl* is written above the base line by one dot.

2 The gradual narrowing of this stroke is achieved by twisting the pen very slightly clockwise.

3, 4 The proportions of initial *'ayn* are dictated by whether it is followed by a descending (3) or an ascending (4) letter.

6 Final joined *kāf* has a different form and proportions from the unjoined one. Compare this joined *kāf* with the large unjoined version on page 15.

5 Initial *kāf*, known as *kāf sayfī* (sword like), followed by different letters.

7 Another initial *kāf*, known as *kāf zannādī* (arm like).

The design of pages 19 to 21 is inspired by calligraphers' practice sheets known in Arabic as *taswīd* (blackening) and in Turkish as *karalama*.

1 Proportions of initial *kāf zannādī*. This *kāf* can also be used as medial.

2 Proportions of medial *kāf sayfī*.

3, 3a Two forms of initial *mīm*.

5, 5a Two forms of medial *mīm*.

4 Final joined *mīm*.

7, 7a The word *ḥamd* (praise) written in two ways using two different medial *mīm*.

6 One way of writing the word *ni^c^mah* (bounty). Notice the varying thicknesses of the strokes and the position of the letters in relation to the base line.

8, 8a Two forms of medial *hā'*.

9 Final joined *hā'*.

10 Another form of medial *hā'*.

1, 1a Two forms of final *hā'* when preceded by the letters *dāl* or *dhāl*.

3, 3a Final *yā'* or final *alif maqṣūrah*.

5 Some of the letters that can join *yā' sayfī* (see 4).

6 Extendable letters. The extended width of any of these letters should be between 9 and 12 dots of the pen.

8, 9 Proportions of *lāmalif* (the letters *lām* and *alif* combined). Some consider *lāmalif* as one letter of the alphabet.

12 Proportions of joined *lāmalif*. See 8 and 9 for unjoined forms.

2 Proportions of one form of medial *hā'*.

4 Variations of final joined *alif maqṣūrah* or *yā'*, known as *yā' sayfī* (sword like) or *yā' rāji*ᶜ*ah* (returning *yā'*).

7 Initial *rā'* known as *rā' raḥmani*. This form of *rā'* cannot be used to write the letter *zay*.

10 Special form reserved for writing the three joined letters of Allah, the name of God. Initial *alif* should be added at the beginning to complete the name.

11 One form of the name of the Prophet Muḥammad.

Stage Three: *Kalimāt* **words**

The Arabic words below have been selected to demonstrate not only all the single unjoined letters of the alphabet, but also many of the variations of joined initial, medial and final letters.

Different pens have been used, hence the variation in size. The fine grey horizontal lines are base line guides. Practise by emulating each word several times until you achieve a satisfactory result.

ذئب منفاخ نبات دار باب

bāb door ***dār*** house ***nabāt*** plant ***minfākh*** blower ***dhi'b*** wolf

دجاج فلاح زمان خطاط

khaṭṭāt calligrapher ***zamān*** time ***fallāḥ*** farmer ***dajāj*** chickens

انسان رياح معروف زقاق

zuqāq alleyway ***maʿrūf*** known ***riyāḥ*** wind ***insān*** human

نباح مشترك قلاع الحكماء

al-ḥukamā' wise men ***qilāʿ*** forts ***mushtarik*** subscriber ***nibāḥ*** barking

محراث قماش راية ناس

nās people ***rāyah*** banner ***qimāsh*** cloth ***miḥrāth*** plough

استيقاظ لصوص اغراض عزم

ʿ***azm*** determination ***aghrāḍ*** purposes ***luṣūṣ*** thieves ***istīqāẓ*** waking up

مهلة كرة وحيد اصباغ

aṣbāgh paints ***waḥīd*** lonely ***kurah*** ball ***muhlah*** period

نادي هدوء سليمان ماء

mā' water **Suleimān** Solomon ***hudū'*** quiet ***nādī*** club

بهجة حماية كتابي بلده

baladahu his country **kitābī** my book **ḥimāyah** protection **bahjah** joy

شريك نشبت المعيشة تيجان ينفخ

yanfakh he is blowing **tījān** crowns **al-maʿīshah** livelihood **nashabat** it erupted **sharīk** partner

جوي يقفز شكر حكمه

ḥikmah wisdom **shukr** thanks **yaqfiz** he is jumping **jawwī** by air

بطلاً صافي مهم اللبن الاعتماد

al-iʿtimād reliance **al-laban** yogurt **muhim** important **ṣāfī** clear **batalan** hero

وَقَوَامُهُ فِي كَثْرَةِ المَشْقِ وَدَوَامِهِ

'Calligraphy is hidden in the teachings of the master, and its betterment lies in ample and continuous practice.'
Attributed to ʿAlī Ibn Abī Ṭālib, the fourth Caliph (d.661)

كمال فائض حرفه نستهلك

nastahlik we consume ***ḥirfah*** profession ***fā'iḍ*** surplus ***kamāl*** perfection

ساحر مستمع ناسخ ينبئني صائغ

ṣā'igh goldsmith ***yunbi'unī*** he notifies me ***nāsikh*** copier ***mustamiᶜ*** listener ***sāḥir*** magician

نتيجة طائش بعدكم مترجم

mutarjim interpreter ***baᶜdakum*** after you ***ṭā'ish*** reckless ***natījah*** result

يتسابق الشجرة قلم خبرتك قبض

qabaḍa he obtained ***khibratuka*** your experience ***qalam*** pen ***al-shajarah*** tree ***yatasābaq*** he is racing

الخطُّ مخفيٌّ في تعليمِ الأستاذِ

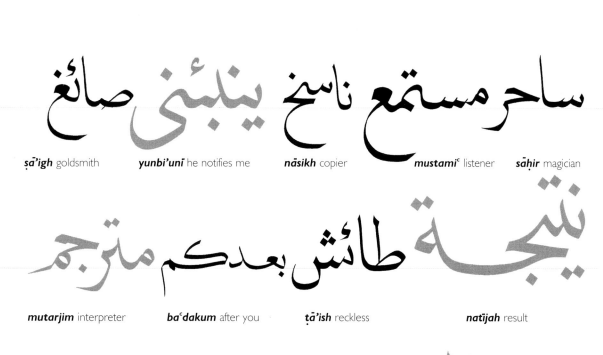

Gallery

Unlike some scripts such as Jalī Thuluth, Tughra and Jalī Dīwānī which have been treated in imaginative and experimental ways, Naskh, a script favoured for its clarity and legibility and therefore sometimes considered 'ordinary', has not in the past been subjected to more individual interpretations. A text in Naskh is usually written to be accessed easily or to be read. Here are some attempts to break with this tradition. The four featured pieces are intended to be primarily visual compositions.

'A man belongs where he settles, and not where he grew up; where he is now, and not where he was born.' Ancient Arabic proverb

The calligraphic works on pages 26 to 29 are by the author.

'The letter is a veil and the veil is a letter.' al-Nuffarī (d.965)

الحرف حجاب والحجاب حرف

'Doubt is the first grade of conviction.' al-Ghazālī (d.1111)

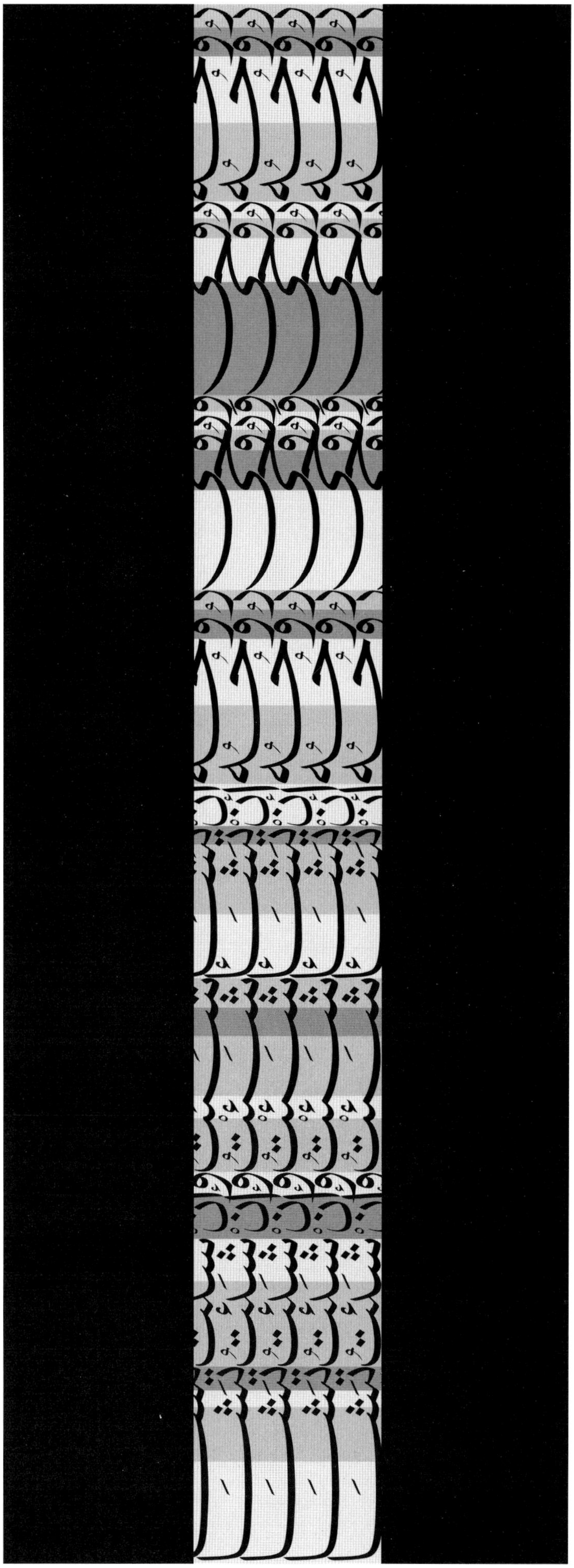

Verse from a poem by al-Ḥallāj (d.922)

Naskh past and present

Naskh is one of the oldest Arabic scripts still in use today. Its survival is due partly to the fact that it is the script used to write the Qur'ān throughout the Islamic world. Its worldwide use has led to the development of many variations.

For centuries novice calligraphers have begun with the practice of Naskh, a tradition which is still maintained. There seems little doubt that the supreme beauty of the script will continue to be appreciated by people from many parts of the world for many years to come.

Following is a selection of pieces in Naskh script, from a variety of periods and places, showing its versatility.

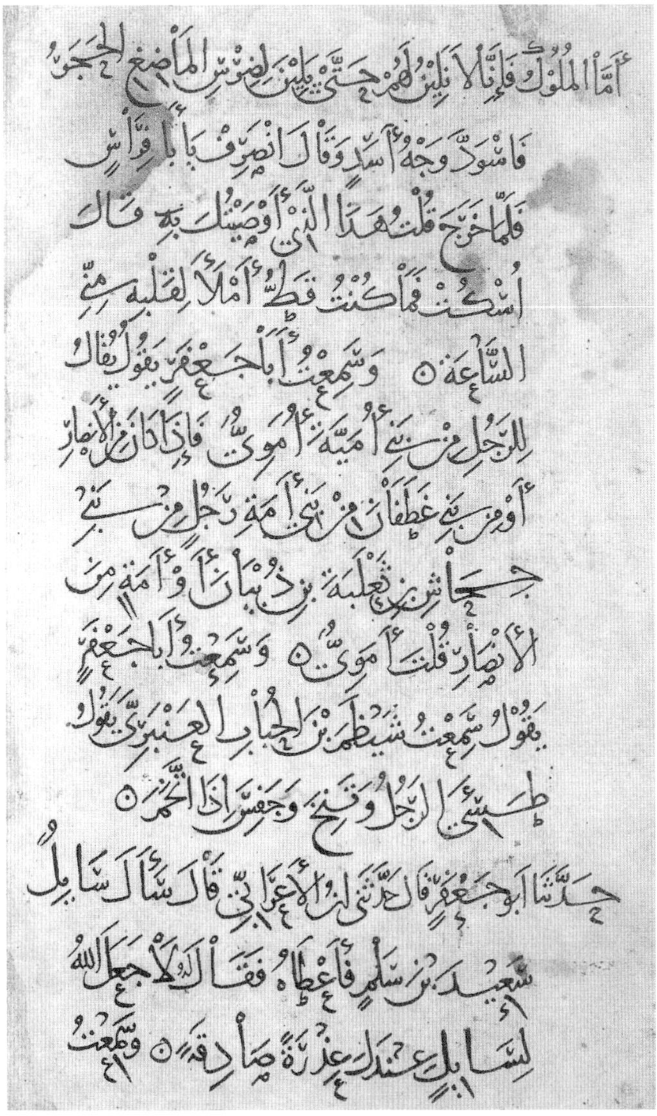

A page from *Kitāb al-Amalī* by Ibn Bābawayh (d.991) written in what is known as Warrāqī script (Naskh-ʿIrāqi) by Muhammad ibn Asad (d.1019 in Baghdad). Ibn Asad was one of the most illustrious calligraphers of his age and master of the famous calligrapher Ibn al-Bawwāb (d.1022).

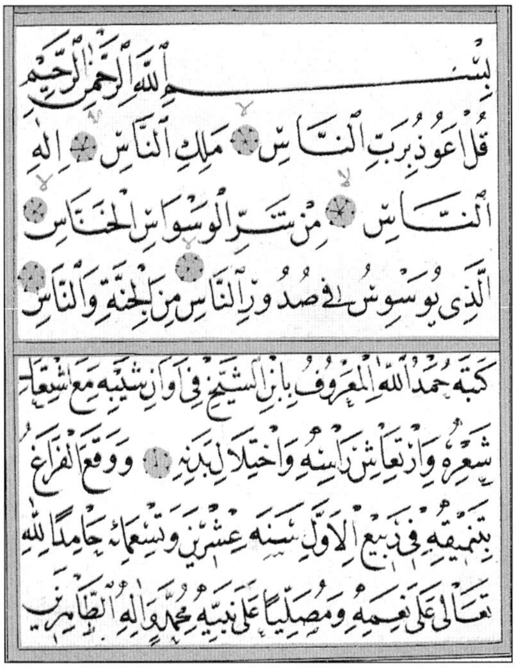

Surah CXIV (*al-Nās*) 'Mankind', and the colophon of a copy of the Qur'ān written in Istanbul by Shaykh Hamdullah (1429-1520). In this copy, which was completed in 1514, the master signed his name with a reference to his grey hair, old age, shaky head and poor health. Shaykh Hamdullah produced forty-seven copies of the Qur'ān in all and was known as *qiblat al-kuttāb*, the calligraphers' lodestar.

Surah I (*al-Fātiḥah*), 'The Opening', from a copy of the Qur'ān written in Istanbul in 1683 by Hafiz Osman (1642-98). Osman, who was the calligraphy master of the Ottoman Sultans Mustafa II and Ahmed III, had developed a Naskh style that is distinguished by its clarity. This style became the standard for those who copied the Qur'ān after him.

A page in Naskh written in a unique way by Aḥmad al-Naīrīzī (Iran?) in 1701/2. The text consists of sixteen lines written in alternating directions. Having read the first set of eight upright lines, the reader has to turn the page upside down to read the remainder. The first eight lines are advice to renounce all forms of earthly pleasure. The remaining eight lines consist of a thirty-word tongue-twisting poem in Arabic with a total of forty initial, medial and final *kāf* letters. It seems that calligraphers of the past loved to test themselves with this particular poem/prayer.

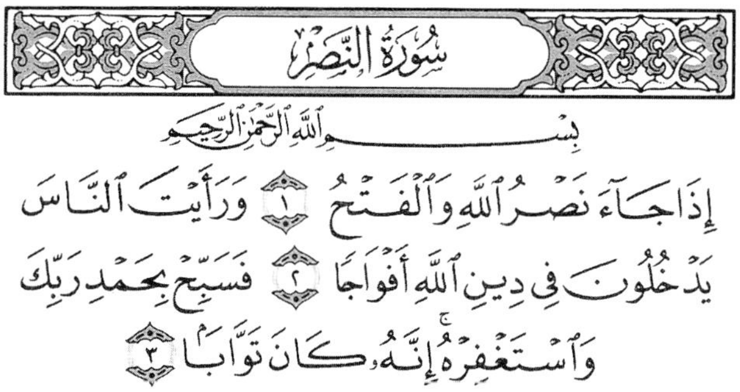

Surah CX (*al-Naṣr*) 'Succour', from a copy of the Qur'ān printed in Saudi Arabia in 1993. It is written in a modern and elegant Naskh by Osman Taha.

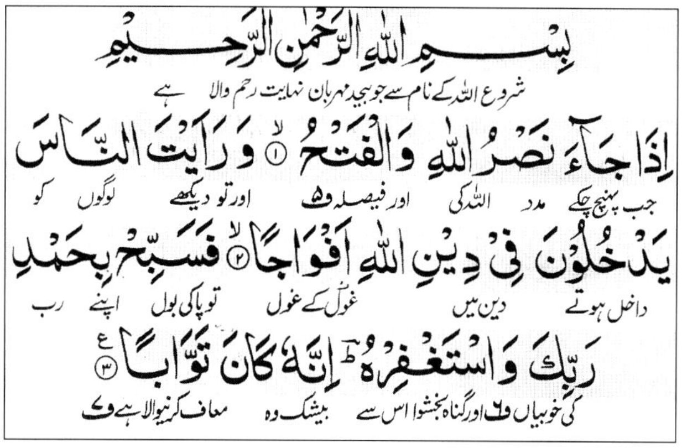

Surah CX (*al-Naṣr*) 'Succour', written in what is known as Indian Naskh, with a translation of the verses in Urdu. This copy of the Qur'ān was printed in Saudi Arabia in 1989 with no reference to the calligrapher's name.

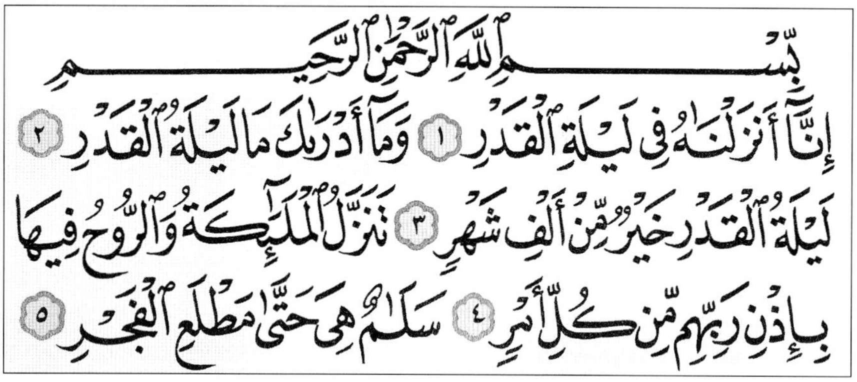

Surah XCVII (*al-Qadr*) 'Predestination', beautifully written in bold modern Naskh that carries vestiges of older styles. This copy of the Qur'ān was printed in Britain. Neither the production date nor the name of the calligrapher is given.

الخَطُّ مخفيٌّ في تعليمِ الأُستاذِ وقوامُهُ في كَثرةِ المَشقِ ودوامُهُ

Arabic desktop publishing fonts based on Naskh script, though functional and widely used, look very rigid and mechanical when compared with handwritten scripts. For this reason new copies of the Qur'ān are still reproduced from originals handwritten by renowned calligraphers and not typeset.

Compare this piece of typesetting with the same sentence written in Naskh across the bottom of pages 24 and 25.

Bibliography

‘Khaṭṭ’
J. Sourdel Thomine *et al.* in
The Encyclopaedia of Islam
(new edition) vol. IV, pp. 1113-28
Leiden, Brill, 1960 ...

Qawāʿid al-Khaṭṭ al-ʿArabī
(Rules of Arabic Calligraphy)
Hāshim Muḥammad al-Khaṭṭāṭ
First published Baghdad, 1960s

Islamic Calligraphy
Yasin Hamid Safadi
Thames and Hudson, London, 1978

Calligraphy and Islamic Culture
A. Schimmel
Hagop Kevorkian Series on Near Eastern Art
and Civilization
New York University Press, New York, 1984

The Early Alphabet
J. Healey
The British Museum Press, London, 1990

Islamic Inscriptions
S. Blair
Edinburgh University Press, Edinburgh, 1998

The Art of Calligraphy in the Islamic Heritage
M. Uğur Derman
and Nihad M. Çetin
The Research Centre for Islamic History,
Art and Culture (IRCICA), Istanbul, 1998

The Sultan’s Signature
Ottoman Calligraphy from the Sakip Sabanci Museum,
Sabanci University, Istanbul
M. Uğur Derman
Deutsche Guggenheim, Berlin, 2001

Illustration acknowledgments

The Research Centre for Islamic History, Art and Culture
(IRCICA), Istanbul:
illustrations on page 30

King Fahad’s Complex for Printing the Holy Qur’ān,
Medina, Saudi Arabia:
two samples of Surah CX (*al-Naṣr*) on page 31

The British Museum, London:
page by Aḥmad al-Nairīzī on page 31

Dār Ibn Qudāmah for Printing and Publishing,
London, Damascus and Beirut:
Surah XCVII (*al-Qadr*) on page 31